STRATEGY AND THE REVOLUTION IN MILITARY AFFAIRS:

FROM THEORY TO POLICY

Steven Metz
James Kievit

June 27, 1995

* * * * * * *

The views expressed in this report are those of the authors and do not necessarily reflect the official policy or position of the Department of the Army, the Department of Defense, or the U.S. Government. This report is cleared for public release; distribution is unlimited.

* * * * * * *

The authors would like to thank Douglas Lovelace, William Johnsen, Douglas Johnson, Gerald Wilkes and Robert Bunker for insightful comments on earlier drafts of this manuscript.

* * * * * * *

Comments pertaining to this report are invited and should be forwarded to: Director, Strategic Studies Institute, U.S. Army War College, Carlisle Barracks, PA 17013-5050. Comments also may be conveyed directly to the authors. Dr. Metz can be contacted at (717) 245-3822, DSN 242-3822, FAX (717) 245-3820, or via Internet at metzs@carlisle-emh2.army.mil. LTC Kievit can be contacted at (717) 245-4140, DSN 242-4140, FAX (717) 245-3820, or via Internet at kievitj@carlisle-emh2.army.mil.

FOREWORD

A small band of "RMA" analysts has emerged in the military and Department of Defense, in the academic strategic studies community, and in defense-related think-tanks and consulting firms. To these analysts, the Gulf War provided a vision of a potential revolution in military affairs (RMA) in which "Information Age" technology would be combined with appropriate doctrine and training to allow a small but very advanced U.S. military to protect national interests with unprecedented efficiency.

In this study, the authors examine the open-source literature on the RMA that has resulted. They find that much of it has concentrated on defining and describing military revolutions and that, despite the efforts of some of the finest minds in the defense analytical community, it has not offered either comprehensive basic theories or broad policy choices and implications.

The authors believe that in order to master a RMA rather than be dragged along by it, Americans must debate its theoretical underpinnings, strategic implications, core assumptions, and normative choices. As a step in that direction they provide a set of hypotheses regarding the configuration and process of revolutions in military affairs, and examine some of their potential policy implications.

The Strategic Studies Institute is pleased to offer this report as a contribution to the informed debate regarding development of a 21st century Army.

RICHARD H. WITHERSPOON
Colonel, U.S. Army
Director, Strategic Studies
    Institute

BIOGRAPHICAL SKETCHES
OF THE AUTHORS

STEVEN METZ is Associate Research Professor of National Security Affairs at the Strategic Studies Institute, U.S. Army War College. He has taught at the Air War College, U.S. Army Command and General Staff College, and several universities. Dr. Metz holds a B.A. and M.A. in international studies from the University of South Carolina, and a Ph.D. in political science from the Johns Hopkins University.

JAMES KIEVIT is a Strategic Research Analyst at the Strategic Studies Institute, U.S. Army War College. Commissioned in the Corps of Engineers, LTC Kievit has served in the 1st Cavalry Division, the 7th Engineer Brigade, and the 8th Infantry Division (Mechanized). He has also served as Assistant Professor of History at the U.S. Military Academy, and as a force structure analyst and study director at the U.S. Army Concepts Analysis Agency. LTC Kievit holds a B.S. from the U.S. Military Academy, a M.M.A.S. from the School of Advanced Military Studies of the U.S. Army Command and General Staff College, and a M.A. in history and M.S.E. in construction management from the University of Michigan.

SUMMARY

Context.

American combat effectiveness in the Gulf War suggested that a historic revolution in military affairs (RMA) is underway, possibly solving many of the strategic dilemmas the United States faces in the post-Cold War world. Inspired by this notion, a small group of RMA analysts has emerged. So far they have concentrated on defining and describing military revolutions. Now broader theoretical and policy issues must be addressed.

Orthodoxy.

The notion of military revolutions grew from Soviet writing of the 1970s and 1980s. Early studies talked of a "military technical revolution" (MTR), but this quickly evolved into the more holistic concept of revolutions in military affairs. Most analysts define a RMA as a "discontinuous increase in military capability and effectiveness" arising from simultaneous and mutually supportive change in technology, systems, operational methods, and military organizations. The current RMA is characterized by four types of changes:

- extremely precise, stand-off strikes;

- dramatically improved command, control, and intelligence;

- information warfare; and

- nonlethality.

Analysts see a number of benefits from harnessing the current revolution in military affairs and using it to build 21st century U.S. armed forces:

- rejuvenating the political utility of military power;

• delaying the emergence of a peer competitor;

• providing a blueprint for technology acquisition and force reorganization; and,

• inspiring conceptual, forward-looking thinking.

Most analysts believe the current RMA will have at least two stages. The first is based on stand-off platforms, stealth, precision, information dominance, improved communications, computers, global positioning systems, digitization, "smart" weapons systems, jointness, and use of ad hoc coalitions. The second may be based on robotics, nonlethality, pyscho-technology, cyberdefense, nanotechnology, "brilliant" weapons systems, hyperflexible organizations, and "fire ant warfare." If this idea is correct, change that has occurred so far will soon be dwarfed by even more fundamental transformation.

Theory.

Strategists who seek to understand and use the revolution in military affairs do not have a mature theory to work from, but need one. The raw materials of theory are hypotheses which can be tested, debated, confirmed, or rejected. Examination of history and the current RMA suggests a number of hypotheses concerning the configuration and process of military revolutions.

Choices.

Key policy decisions made now will affect both the pace of revolution and the shape of the 21st century U.S. military that emerges from it. Perhaps the most fundamental choice of all concerns the enthusiasm with which the United States should pursue the current "minor" RMA and the extent to which it should shape force development.

A case can be made that the costs and risks of vigorous pursuit of the current RMA outweigh the expected benefits. These include risk that:

- the current RMA will not generate increased combat effectiveness against the most likely or most dangerous future opponents;

- American pursuit of the RMA will encourage opponents or potential opponents to seek countermeasures;

- the current RMA might lead the United States toward overreliance on military power; and,

- vigorous pursuit of the current RMA might increase problems with friends and allies.

There are even more pressing reasons supporting U.S. pursuit of the current RMA:

- it should bring significant increases in combat effectiveness against some mid-level opponents;

- a force built around stand-off, precision weapons and disruptive information warfare capabilities would be more politically usable than a traditional force-projection military;

- the RMA could augment deterrence; and,

- the United States may need to pursue the current RMA to avoid stumbling into strategic inferiority.

If policymakers decide to pursue the revolution in military affairs, strategy, rather than technological capability should guide force development. The key question is: What do we want the future U.S. military to be able to do?" The answer depends on broad strategic objectives and expected opponents.

In terms of strategic objectives, the more the United States stresses active engagement and the promulgation of open economies and political systems, the more the U.S. military must be able to project power and sustain protracted operations. The more that the United States pursues political and military disengagement, the less the need for power projection or sustained operations. At this end of the spectrum, the appropriate military force would be configured for defense and short deterrent strikes.

Force development must also be driven by some projected priority among the threat types. Most current programs, including the Army's Force XXI, focus on conventional regional aggressors and, to a lesser extent, subnational enemies. From this perspective, stress on precision, stand-off strikes, stealth, and coherent operations is logical. But if the future threat set changes, these characteristics might not be the most important ones for the future U.S. military.

A peer competitor with armed forces as advanced as the U.S. military (although perhaps not in precisely the same way) could pose entirely different problems. To attempt projection of conventional forces against a peer competitor would be exceedingly dangerous, perhaps impossible. Under conditions of direct confrontation with a peer competitor, the United States should concentrate on projection of effects rather than objects. Against a peer competitor, the United States would certainly need a tightly integrated military-scientific-technological-economic policy aimed at limiting the proliferation of military-relevant knowledge.

A U.S. military configured for use against subnational or nonmilitary enemies would be composed of small but very flexible units (but the force as a whole might not be small). The entire combat arms component of the Army might be composed of Special Forces. High-tech policemen and scientists, whether computer experts, ecologists, or something similar would be the most vital parts of the security force with soldiers as adjuncts. Personal protection technology including individual armor and counterterror technology would be essential. Psychotechnology to manipulate perceptions, beliefs and attitudes would also be central.

Tasks.

The RMA is at a crossroads. In the broadest sense, there are three options:

- push further along the road of precision, stand-off strikes and disruptive information warfare aimed primarily at conventionally-armed regional aggressors;

- put a brake on the RMA and stand pat in order to consolidate existing advantages; or,

- push the revolution in a different direction.

To structure the choice among these options, the U.S. military must inspire and lead continued refinement of the theory of military revolutions, cultivate internal creativity, and expand debate on the RMA outside the military and defense community. It is particularly important to consider the normative dimension of strategy. American leaders must decide not only what the United States *can* do with a more effective military force, but also what it *should* do. Only then will the RMA lead to progress rather than simply change.

STRATEGY AND THE REVOLUTION
IN MILITARY AFFAIRS:
FROM THEORY TO POLICY

Context.

American combat effectiveness in the Gulf War amazed observers around the world. Out of Iraq and Kuwait came hints of a future where the U.S. military could strike anywhere with force, precision, and relative safety, its enemies electronically confused into submission with little of warfare's normal collateral destruction. It seemed that "information age" technology, if combined with appropriate doctrine and training, might allow a small but advanced 21st century U.S. military to protect national interests with unprecedented efficiency. The Gulf War thus suggested that a historic revolution in military affairs (RMA) is underway, bringing solutions to many of the strategic dilemmas of the post-Cold War world.

This heady vision aroused tremendous excitement among American defense planners. Given the requirement in current U.S. military strategy to fight two nearly simultaneous "major regional contingencies" in the face of rapidly declining force size, increased effectiveness at reduced cost has become an obsession.[1] To attain it requires breaking old intellectual fetters. Consequently, seldom in American history have military leaders and defense planners been more open to new ideas. This holds even at the highest levels-Admiral William A. Owens, Vice Chairman of the Joint Chiefs of Staff, has posted a public message on the Internet providing his electronic mail address and stating, "I'd like to open a dialogue on a few subjects that I think are important and solicit your ideas . . . what is the impact of the ongoing technology revolution and what does this mean in terms of our strategy, our doctrine, our command structures, etc?"[2]

From this blend of urgency and exploration, a small band of RMA analysts emerged in the military and Department of

Defense, the academic strategic studies community, and defense-related think-tanks and consulting firms. Although this group includes some brilliant thinkers, its output so far has not been theoretically comprehensive and, as a result, has offered only limited policy choices. Since the RMA is a relatively new concept to Western strategic thinkers, much of the writing has concentrated on defining and describing military revolutions and possible future capabilities. Now is the time to push the analysis to new levels. Andrew W. Marshall contends the "longer term questions and issues" concerning goals and strategy "should be addressed."[3] If anything, this is an understatement—they *must* be addressed.

Military preeminence without an appropriate strategy to shape and utilize it is both dangerous and fleeting. Yet crafting such a strategy for the RMA is more difficult than simply developing and applying technology. Americans are pragmatic. Faced with the rush of day-to-day problems in a complex and dangerous security environment, American strategists often overlook the assumptions and concepts that undergird their actions, focusing on short-term programs rather than long-term goals. This can be hazardous. To master the RMA rather than be dragged along by it, Americans must now debate its theoretical underpinnings, strategic implications, core assumptions, and normative choices, all as preface to the formulation of cogent policy.

Orthodoxy.

The notion of military revolutions grew from Soviet writing of the 1970s and 1980s, particularly a series of papers by Marshal N.V. Ogarkov analyzing the revolutionary potential of new military technologies.[4] As Marxists, Ogarkov and his colleagues were comfortable with the idea that history is driven by revolutions. When American defense analysts, more familiar with scientific revolutions than Hegelian and Marxist revolutions of consciousness, did turn to military revolutions they also initially focused on the technology. Early studies talked of a "military technical revolution" (MTR).[5] But analysts quickly found an exclusively technological focus too limiting and the MTR evolved into the more holistic concept of revolutions in military affairs.[6] The first step, then, was agreement that something revolutionary might be underway or impending.[7]

The second step is harder. As could be expected with a dramatically new idea, analysts of the RMA have not fully agreed on its meaning. Futurists Alvin and Heidi Toffler, for instance, use a restrictive definition based on macro-level economic structure. They write:

> A military revolution, in the fullest sense, occurs only when a new civilization arises to challenge the old, when an entire society transforms itself, forcing its armed services to change at every level simultaneously–from technology and culture to organization, strategy, tactics, training, doctrine, and logistics. When this happens, the relationship of the military to the economy and society is transformed and the military balance of power on earth is shattered.[8]

From this grand perspective, there have been only two true military revolutions, the first associated with the rise of organized, agricultural society, and the second with the industrial revolution. Robert Bunker has offered an equally large-scale schema based on the "energy foundation" of war.[9]

Most analysts addressing the RMA, though, have adopted less inclusive and restrictive definitions stressing a "discontinuous increase in military capability and effectiveness."[10] According to Andrew Krepinevich, a military revolution:

> ... occurs when the application of new technologies into a significant number of military systems combines with innovative operational concepts and organizational adaptation in a way that fundamentally alters the character and conduct of conflict. It does so by producing a dramatic increase–often an order of magnitude or greater–in the combat potential and military effectiveness of armed forces.[11]

Analysts have concluded that a revolution in military affairs dramatically increases combat effectiveness by four types of simultaneous and mutually supportive change: technological change; systems development; operational innovation; and, organizational adaptation.[12] The relative priority among these elements varies from revolution to revolution. The current revolution, for instance, is heavily shaped by technology.

In general, analysts agree more on the defining characteristics and components of the *current* RMA than on military revolutions in general. One such defining characteristic is the alteration of the relationship of accuracy and distance in the application of military force. Traditionally, accuracy diminished with distance. At certain times technology has dramatically altered this relationship by extending the distance at which fires could be accurate. The invention of the compound bow was one such time, as was the widespread rifling of small arms, the invention of recoil mechanisms for rifled artillery, the development of strategic bombing and close air support, and the invention of guided missiles. To some extent, accuracy still diminishes with distance, but emerging technology has made extremely precise, stand-off strikes possible. Some analysts now see stand-off strikes as a replacement for close-range encounters rather than an adjunct to them. "Stealthy long-range precision strike," according to James R. Fitzsimonds and Jan M. Van Tol, "may become the dominant operational approach."[13]

Precise, stand-off conventional strikes, however complex, are the least radical of the military capabilities associated with the current RMA. Much of the requisite technology is fielded or will be soon. The second defining characteristic of the current RMA—an increasing interest in information warfare—represents a greater departure from tradition. Information has always been a vital part of war, whether in the form of intelligence or psychological operations. Analysts now predict that technology will dramatically improve command, control, and intelligence. This will alter the traditional relationship between operational complexity and effective control as electronic, sometimes space-based, methods for acquiring, analyzing, and disseminating information allow military activity to be much more complex than in the past and still remain timely, synchronized, and controllable. Simultaneous operations are now possible across a military theater of operations under some circumstances. Maturation of the current RMA may make them possible under all conditions and across several theaters of operations.

But analysts view information as more than simply a tool for operational control, and increasingly consider it a strategic asset. This is a seminal change, reflecting Alvin and Heidi Toffler's contention that information is becoming the basis of economic strength, especially in what they call "Third Wave" states.[14] During the "First Wave" of human development, production was primarily agricultural, so war sought to seize and hold territory. During the "Second Wave," industrial production dominated, so war was often a struggle of attrition where belligerents wore down their enemy's capacity to feed, clothe, and equip armies. Following this logic, "Third Wave" warfare will seek to erode or destroy the enemy's means of collecting, processing, storing, and disseminating information. Since the more dependent an enemy is on information the more vulnerable it would be to information warfare, this would seem to have potential as a counter to an advanced, peer threat.

So far, though, no consensus on information warfare's strategic or operational implications has emerged.[15] Many analysts within the military and Department of Defense have viewed information warfare as an adjunct to conventional strikes-a force multiplier-rather than a stand-alone method of warfare.[16] There has been some discussion of the potential strategic implications of information warfare among the military and its associated defense community, but only a few writers have proposed even the beginning of a comprehensive framework for the strategic utilization of such warfare.[17]

A third defining characteristic of the current RMA is a reduction in both casualties and the collateral damage normally associated with military combat operations. Partly this will result from precision conventional strikes. But even more radical change may be possible through nonlethality. Chris and Janet Morris have provided some of the most systematic analysis of what they call "weapons of mass protection" which are electromagnetic, kinetic, or nonlethal chemical devices "that can be used earlier to deter by denial in order to support diplomacy, to limit aggression, to nonlethally disarm or dissuade, and to destroy lethal capability with a minimum of damage to noncombatants, combatants, and the environment."[18] Examples include acoustic, laser and high power microwaves, nonnuclear electromagnetic pulses, high power jamming, obscurants, foams, glues and slicks, supercaustics, magnetohydrodynamics, information warfare, and soldier protection. Since the Gulf War, interest by the U.S. military in such nonlethal arms has increased.[19] By 1995, U.S. forces involved in peace operations deployed with early versions of some of them.[20] In fact, nonlethal weapons would seem to have their greatest applicability in conflict short of war. The full policy implications of nonlethality, though, are still under exploration.[21]

Analysts see a number of benefits from harnessing the current revolution in military affairs and using it to build 21st century U.S. armed forces. One of the most widely discussed is a rejuvenation of the political utility of military power. Due to instantaneous global communications, the pervasiveness of the electronic media, and the low American tolerance for casualties, force seems to have become less usable just as the U.S. military attained clear global preeminence. Most RMA analysts consider intolerance of casualties the key variable; nonlethal weapons may offer the solution. "Given the performance of certain modern weapons," Edward Luttwak writes, "if military planning is appropriately modified to fully exploit their technical potential, it may be possible to emulate the casualty-avoiding methods of eighteenth-century warfare and thus conduct armed yet virtually bloodless interventions."[22] Nonlethal weapons might allow the world community to intervene earlier in a crisis when a solution is more attainable or, at least, attainable at a lower cost. Falling somewhere between a show of force and conventional military intervention, "disabling weapons could provide a deterrent prior to crisis development or could diffuse the crisis before it expands."[23] If military action is bloody, it becomes a last resort. But used only when conflicts have become nearly intractable, it has the least chance of success. The argument is sometimes made, for instance, that a multinational peacekeeping force armed largely with nonlethal weaponry might have been able to prevent the conflict in Bosnia from escalating to outright war-a little force applied early in a crisis is better than extensive force applied later.

In addition to augmenting the political utility of military power, the RMA might allow the United States to preserve the margin of military superiority it now has by delaying the emergence of a peer competitor.[24] Presumably other states would recognize and eschew the immense cost of catching up and then keeping pace with a United States that is improving an already-preeminent military. Some analysts—most persuasively Michael Mazarr—argue that the RMA can also provide guidelines for constructing a post-Cold War U.S. national security strategy, suggesting which of the various emerging technologies should be pursued and how the armed forces should be organized and trained.[25] Perhaps most importantly, the RMA, by introducing American defense planners to the notion of historic military revolutions, can spark conceptual, forward-looking thinking. Andrew Krepinevich, following Marx, argues that what distinguishes revolution from evolution is recognition and acceptance of fundamental change by those involved.[26]

Many analysts agree on one other important fact: the current revolution in military affairs seems to have at least two stages (see Figure 1). In the drive to limit military casualties, stand-off platforms, stealth, precision, information dominance, and missile defense are the first stage. The second may be robotics, nonlethality, pyschotechnology, and elaborate cyberdefense. The revolution in military affairs may see the transition from concern with centers of gravity to a less mechanistic and more sophisticated notion of interlinked systems.[27] For coordination, the first stage is improved communications, computers, global positioning systems, digitization, and "smart" weapons systems. The second stage may be nanotechnology which allows the dispersion of thousands of tiny intelligence-gathering machines and "brilliant" weapons systems able to make sophisticated decisions about when and how to act. To organize for the RMA, the first stage is composed of joint task forces and ad hoc coalitions. This may be followed by a uniservice or non-service structure for the U.S. military, abolition of the reserves (or

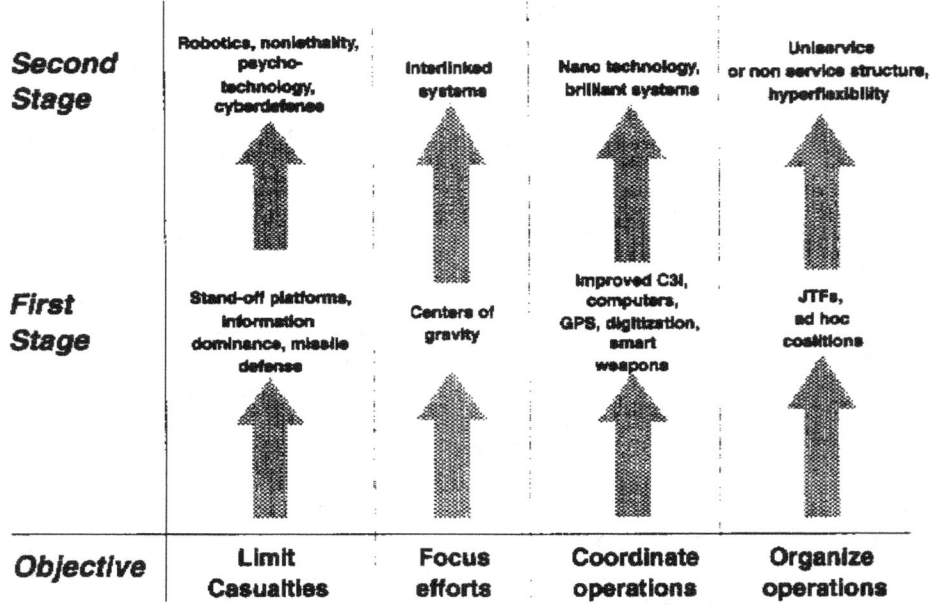

	Limit Casualties	Focus efforts	Coordinate operations	Organize operations
Second Stage	Robotics, nonlethality, psycho-technology, cyberdefense	Interlinked systems	Nano technology, brilliant systems	Uniservice or non service structure, hyperflexiblity
First Stage	Stand-off platforms, information dominance, missile defense	Centers of gravity	Improved C3I, computers, GPS, digitization, smart weapons	JTFs, ad hoc coalitions
Objective	**Limit Casualties**	**Focus efforts**	**Coordinate operations**	**Organize operations**

Figure 1. Stages of the Current Revolution.

abolition of standing forces), hyperflexible organizations, and what Martin Libicki calls "fire ant warfare" in which a web of millions of small, smart weapons swarm on a target.[28] If this two stage idea is correct, change that has occurred so far will soon be dwarfed by even more fundamental transformation. Most analysts thus conclude that the world is only at the beginning of the current military revolution.[29]

Theory.

Even though the revolution in military affairs has attracted some brilliant thinkers, systematic strategic discourse remains rare. Except for Andrew Krepinevich and Jeffrey Cooper, few writers have attempted to place the current RMA in its broader theoretic and historic context. While many writers admit that larger questions need answers, the normal approach is t o assume continuity in the global security environment and t o approach the RMA programmatically. This is understandable. Faced with the crush of day-to-day issues and problems, strategists and security planners sometimes overlook the importance of theory to policy. Targeteers in the Strategic Air Command (SAC) designing the Single Integrated Operational Plan might not have been familiar with the theory of nuclear war that coalesced in the 1950s and 1960s, but their work reflected it. The planners of *Desert Storm* might not have thought consciously of Clausewitz as they developed courses of action, but the Prussian's theories permeated their work. And, diplomats hammering out a new treaty might not explicitly consider the theory of international politics that undergirds their efforts, but its impact is there nonetheless.

Unlike planners in SAC, Central Command, or the Department of State, strategists who seek to understand and use the revolution in military affairs do not have a mature theory to work from, but need one. Theory-building is a collaborative effort involving a community of analysts and scholars. Its raw materials are hypotheses which can be tested, debated, confirmed, or rejected. For the RMA, there are a number of feasible ways to group such hypotheses, but one that seems to make sense is by *configuration* and *process*.

Configuration (Figure 2). Both the Tofflers, who identify only two historical military revolutions, and Krepinevich, who distinguishes ten since the 14th century, are correct if the theory is broad enough to account for both "major" and "minor" revolutions in military affairs. "Minor" RMAs like the division and corps organization of Napoleonic armies and the incorporation of rifled weapons in the 19th century were constituent parts of a "major" revolution which included fundamental social, economic, and political change rather than simply a radical increase in combat effectiveness.[30] "Minor" RMAs can be shaped and controlled by those who understand them. "Major" revolutions cannot be controlled; strategists must respond and adapt to them. Not every "minor" revolution must be pursued in order to remain a viable actor in the international military arena, but the "major" revolutions in military affairs cannot be ignored. In the past, individual circumstance permitted nations, without inordinate strategic risk, to choose not to build amphibious warfare capabilities, create panzer armies, or adopt Maoist "people's war." But every nation desiring to

- There ar "major" and "minor" revolutions in military affairs.

- "Minor" revolutions in military affairs tend to be initiated by individual technological or social changes, occur in relatively short periods (less than a decade), and have their greatest direct impact on the battlefield.

- "Major" revolutions in military affairs are the result of combined multiple technological, economic, social, cultural and/or military changes, usually occur over relatively long periods (greater that a decade), and have direct impact on strategy.

- "Minor" revolutions in military affairs can be deliberately shaped and controlled; "Major" revolutions cannot.

- A "minor" revolution in military affairs driven by military applications of silicon-chip technology is underway, and the next "minor" revolution will be driven by robotics and psychotechnology.

- In the future, "minor" revolutions in military affairs will occur closer together than in the past, almost to the point of continuous revolution.

- The world is potentially at the beginning of a "major" revolution in military affairs resulting from the interaction of multiple economic, social, and cultural changes driven by silicon-chip, robotic, psycho- and bio-technologies.

- The increase in combat effectiveness due to sequential revolutions in military affairs has tended to be cumulative, but effectiveness is always a relative -- not an absolute -- measurement.

- Revolutions in military affairs, while increasing some aspects of combat effectiveness, may either decrease or increase the strategic utility of the military element of power.

**Figure 2. Hypotheses on the Configuration
on Revolutions in Military Affairs.**

remain a strategic player was forced to adopt some form of mass military backed by industrial capacity or the ability to acquire manufactured goods.

The increase in combat effectiveness associated with revolutions in military affairs is cumulative. Since the collapse of the Roman Empire, there has been no instance of reversion to pre-revolutionary levels. While the aggregate change may vary, the trend in combat effectiveness has been steadily upward, with short periods of intense movement (revolutions) and longer periods of evolutionary development (see Figure 3).

Still, combat effectiveness is always relative. Percussion-cap rifled muskets of the mid-19th century were certainly more effective than flintlock smoothbores. Against poorly armed tribesmen who were their primary adversaries, the rifle-armed British military of the Victorian Age possessed a decisive advantage. Against similarly equipped forces o f potential European opponents, however, British effectiveness decreased because superior training and discipline no longer

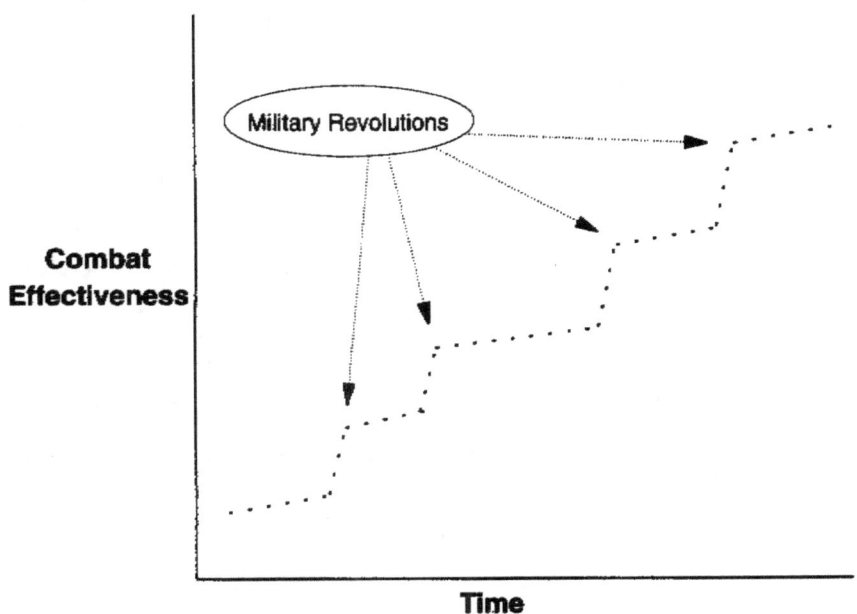

Figure 3. Effectiveness and Revolutions.

provided as significant an edge against an opponent who could engage at much greater range.[31] Effectiveness, then, deals with a *relationship* between real or potential enemies.

Furthermore, increased weapon system effectiveness does not automatically translate into increased utility for military power as a strategic instrument. In the American Civil War, rifle-equipped infantry was more effective against other arms, but unable to force a decision against similarly equipped opposing infantry. Since, as Russell Weigley notes, "the military commander in quest of decisiveness needs an effective arm of mobile war," the increased effectiveness of infantry against cavalry combined with infantry's inability to maneuver against rifle-equipped enemy infantry actually *degraded* the strategic utility of tactical engagements.[32] This made the conflict's outcome depend more upon other considerations than on the direct application of military power.

Process (Figure 4). Revolutions in military affairs appear to follow a cyclical pattern with initial stasis followed by initiation, critical mass, consolidation, response, and return to stasis (see

- Revolutions in military affairs are cyclical processes.

- Revolutions in military affairs can be initiated by one breakthrough power or by a group.

- In the modern security system, revolutions in military affairs are usually inspired by outright defeat, or by a perception of inferiority or decline versus a peer or niche opponent.

- Initiating a revolution in military affairs requires the empowerment of visionaries.

- Revolutions in military affairs have a point of critical mass when changes in concepts, organizations, and technology meld.

- Once recognized, every revolutionary breakthrough generates responses.

- Responses to revolutions in military affairs can be symmetric or asymmetric; asymmetric responses may be more difficult to counter.

- The greatest advantage for the breakthrough power lies in the period immediately following critical mass; thus there may be a temptation to initiate conflict before responses can be effective.

- All revolutions in military affairs have a culminating point determined by the interaction between the revolutionary breakthrough and the responses, followed by a consolidations phase.

- During the consolidation phase, superior training and leadership may be the only ways to achieve superior relative combat effectiveness against symmetric responses.

- During the consolidation phase, strategic advantage lies with entities best able to employ politico-economic, as opposed to strictly military, power.

**Figure 4. Hypotheses on the Process
of Revolutions in Military Affairs.**

Figure 5). At times, a single state can initiate revolution by recognizing how to effectively combine various evolutionary developments, new ideas, and technology. Napoleonic France and the Mongols of Genghis Khan were examples of single state breakthroughs. At other times, there can be a collective breakthrough as when the European powers of the mid-19th to early 20th centuries combined industrialization, railroads, improved metallurgy and explosives, the telegraph, barbed wire, concrete, improved methods of government funding, nationalism, breech loading, rifled artillery and small arms, steam-driven, armored ships, internal combustion engines, radio, increased literacy and public health, improved explosives, and the machine gun. Always, though, the essence of the revolution is not the invention of new technology, but discovery of innovative ways to organize, operate, and employ new technology.

Revolutions in military affairs begin when the potential latent in technological, conceptual, political, economic, social, and organizational changes that have occurred or are

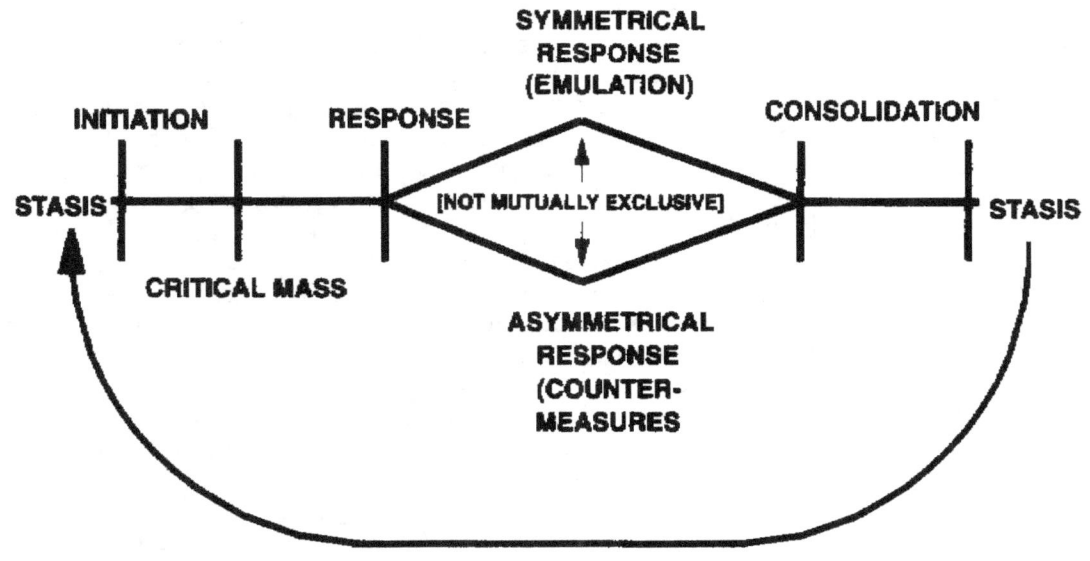

Figure 5. Pattern of Military Revolutions.

occurring is recognized and converted to augment combat effectiveness. In pre-modern, heterogeneous security systems, revolution was often initiated by states outside the system or on its periphery. Sometimes their advantage accrued from superior morale, training, organization, leadership, strategy, or tactics. Examples include Alexander's Macedonians, early Republican Rome, 8th century Arabs, Mongols, Vikings, and the Swedes of Gustavus Adolphus. The Assyrians were perhaps typical when they unleashed a military revolution without new technology—many societies had iron weapons and compound bows—but based on combined arms tactics that integrated archers, spearmen, and charioteers.[33] Other external or peripheral revolutionaries such as the iron-armed Hittites and chariot-riding Kassites, Hurrians, and Hyskos who challenged Mesopotamia and Egypt, or the European conquerors of the Americas, Asia, and Africa did capitalize on superior technology, but did not attain victory purely because of it.[34]

In the modern, communications-intensive security system, revolutions in military affairs have most frequently been initiated by a state within the system. The motivating force often has been defeat, a perception of inferiority, or a fear of declining capability against evolutionary change on the part of other actors. This is because fundamental change of any kind is difficult, even frightening; those who unleash revolution never know exactly where it will take them. Uncertainty as to the eventual outcome means that political and military leaders satisfied with their state's security situation will seldom run the risks of revolution. Usually, then, only real or imagined danger can provide the spark. Revolutionary France, for instance, unleashed a military revolution via the *levee en mass* primarily because it was surrounded with powerful enemies and on the verge of catastrophe. Europe's conservative monarchies repudiated Paris' radical ideology, therefore rejected diplomatic amelioration of the security threat, and possessed superior traditional military capabilities. Military innovation was thus the only alternative left to the beleaguered revolutionaries. In the late 19th century, Britain, Germany, France, and, to a lesser extent, Russia and Austria-Hungary, pursued land and naval military revolutions from fear of each other. Similarly, the

Germans developed *blitzkrieg* between 1918 and 1940 because they recognized that their political objectives were unlikely to be attained without war, and they could not win such a war with available military capabilities.[35]

Initiation of a revolution requires revolutionaries. RMAs are led by armed forces that tolerate and, at the appropriate time, empower visionaries. The decision to do this is a vital juncture in military revolutions. In the past, only a peer competitor could offer enough of a threat to empower military visionaries and dispel the miasma of inertia and petrified thinking. This may be changing. In the future, the United States might face real threats from "niche" challengers that cannot match American capability across the board, but can in some specific type of conflict, perhaps terrorism. Actually niche challengers have always existed, but were often overshadowed. In the post-Cold War security environment, the absence of a peer threat gives niche challengers greater strategic significance, both real and perceptual. Phrased differently, niche threats will be considered important if they are the only type around, but will return to relative insignificance if a peer competitor emerges.

Even when political and military leaders commit their state to radical innovation and empower visionaries, they almost never begin with a complete and clear blueprint for revolution. False starts and dead ends are the rule rather than the exception. In every RMA, though, there is a point of *critical mass* where concepts, organizations, and technologies ripen and meld. For a military revolution to reach critical mass, some factor must protect the breakthrough state while it changes concepts, reorganizes, and wanders down dead ends. Most often, this is division or ignorance on the part of its enemies. These enemies may not recognize the potential danger the breakthrough poses, or may be wandering down dead ends of their own. While Germany developed *blitzkrieg*, for instance, France refined preparation for the set-piece battle to an art form.[36]

The period between initiation and critical mass may be short, particularly when the revolution frees latent creativity within the armed forces and defense community rather than generating it from scratch. The periods immediately before and after critical mass may be particularly conflict-prone as other states recognize the coming danger posed by the breakthrough and attempt to preempt it or the breakthrough state tests its new-found prowess. Often small wars confirm the course of innovation, add fuel to the revolutionary spark, and pave the way for even more extensive change. This happened with the Crimean War, the Franco-Prussian War, and the Russo-Japanese War. Many analysts contend that the Gulf War will play the same role.[37]

Regardless of the reason for initiation or the time and means required to achieve critical mass, revolutionary breakthroughs eventually generate responses from other states. Responses can be symmetric, asymmetric, or, most often, a combination of the two. Symmetric responses seek to emulate the breakthrough state. Prussian military reforms following the Battle of Jena were a classic example.[38] So, too, was the development of the German battle fleet after the appointment of Rear Admiral Alfred Tirpitz as State Secretary in 1897.[39] Following their near-defeat by German *blitzkrieg* in 1941-42, the Soviets emulated the *Wehrmacht's* methods, eventually beating the masters at their own game. Asymmetric responses, by contrast, seek countermeasures to the breakthrough. They are to the process of force and doctrine development what Liddell Hart's "indirect approach" or Edward Luttwak's concept of "paradoxical logic" is to strategy.[40] To counter British battleships, for instance, both the French and Germans focused, at different times and with differing enthusiasm, on submarines, torpedo boats, and fast commerce raiders. The strategy of guerrilla "people's war" as developed by Mao, Giap, and others is perhaps the starkest illustration of an asymmetric approach to a superior military. In today's Third World, the drive for weapons of mass destruction is, in part, an attempt to find asymmetric countermeasures to American conventional military preeminence.

Responses to future military breakthroughs will be quicker than in the past. Before the modern age, it could take decades, even centuries before effective responses emerged. There was always a period where other states simply did not understand the breakthrough followed by a time when they understood the revolutionary concepts, but had not yet adjusted their organization, doctrine, training, attitudes, and technology. In the 21st century, the quantum increase in the pace of organizational adaptation and the extent of global communication will make the advantages flowing from revolutionary breakthrough fleeting. The revolutionary cycle, in other words, will be compressed. Future RMAs will occur in such rapid sequence that military affairs will appear to be in "permanent revolution" (to misappropriate Trostsky's phrase).

The period following critical mass, but before effective response, is a time of greatest relative advantage for the revolutionary power. If conflict with other states arises during this period, it will frequently seem to be in the revolutionary power's best interests to resort to military action immediately. Thus, unless the political and military leaders of the breakthrough state possess self-discipline and demonstrate restraint, this period is susceptible to armed conflict as the breakthrough state launches strategic spoiling attacks.[41]

Military revolutions have *culminating points* at which innovation and change slow or stop. This may occur when leaders become satisfied with the military balance and will no longer risk radical change. It may also occur when costs of change are thought to outweigh the benefits of further expenditure. At this time, states which have adopted the revolution seek to consolidate their advantage. Following culmination, remaining improvements in military effectiveness come primarily through superior training. This the reason that, following nearly universal adoption of the gunpowder-bayonet tactical revolution by 18th century European militaries, Frederick the Great was able to dominate the battlefield. And, it could be argued that American effectiveness in *Desert Storm* represented superior training during the last phase of the *blitzkrieg* RMA.

The most successful revolutionary states turn military advantage into economic and political dominance, but the transition is difficult. Being the first to understand or implement a RMA does not guarantee even military victory. A breakthrough state or coalition which clearly understands the RMA but which fails to develop an appropriate, balanced, strategy can-and usually will-lose to a state or coalition which lags in understanding but possesses superior strategic prowess. History is littered with breakthrough military states which ultimately failed, whether those of Genghis Khan, Napoleon Bonaparte, or Imperial and Nazi Germany. In general, then, leaders and strategists attempting to master military revolutions face a series of key decisions:

- Should the RMA be pursued?

- What is the appropriate pace of change?

- Which path of change should be taken?

- How can the culminating point of the revolution be recognized and what should be done when it is reached? and,

- How can increased combat effectiveness be turned into strategic gain?

Choices.

The course of the current RMA is not preordained. Key policy decisions made now will both affect the pace of revolution and the shape of the 21st century U.S. military that emerges from it. Perhaps the most fundamental choice of all concerns the enthusiasm with which the United States should pursue the current "minor" RMA and the extent to which it should shape force development. Often this is not even considered due to the traditional American approach to technology. The American ethos holds that progress-defined, in part, as efficiency augmented by technology-is inevitable and irrepressible. Technology is respected, almost deified. There are sound historical reasons for this. During its formative period, the nation suffered from chronic shortages of skilled labor, thus forcing reliance on labor-saving technology. Eli Whitney, Robert Fulton, Thomas Edison, Henry Ford and thousands of other entrepreneurs and inventors harnessed technology in the name of efficiency. Reflecting this legacy, the U.S. military has often evinced an unreflective trust in the ultimate benefit of technology. But a reasonable case can be made that too vigorous pursuit of the current "minor" RMA i s undesirable or dangerous, that the costs and risks outweigh the expected benefits.

One risk is that the current RMA, if it continues on its present trajectory, will not generate increased combat effectiveness against the most likely or most dangerous future opponents. The "perfect" opponent for an military structured around the current RMA is a "middle level" enemy with rigid, centralized decisionmaking relying on limited range, easy-to-detect weapons platforms such as tanks, conventional artillery, and manned aircraft. But the utility of the current RMA, with its stress on precision, stand-off strikes, falls off dramatically toward the poles of the military/technology spectrum (see Figure 6). Opponents at the low end of the spectrum tend to operate in widely dispersed fashion and emit a limited electronic signature, thus complicating targeting.[42] Their organization is often cellular, making decapitation difficult. If they are insurgents, they intermingle with the population,

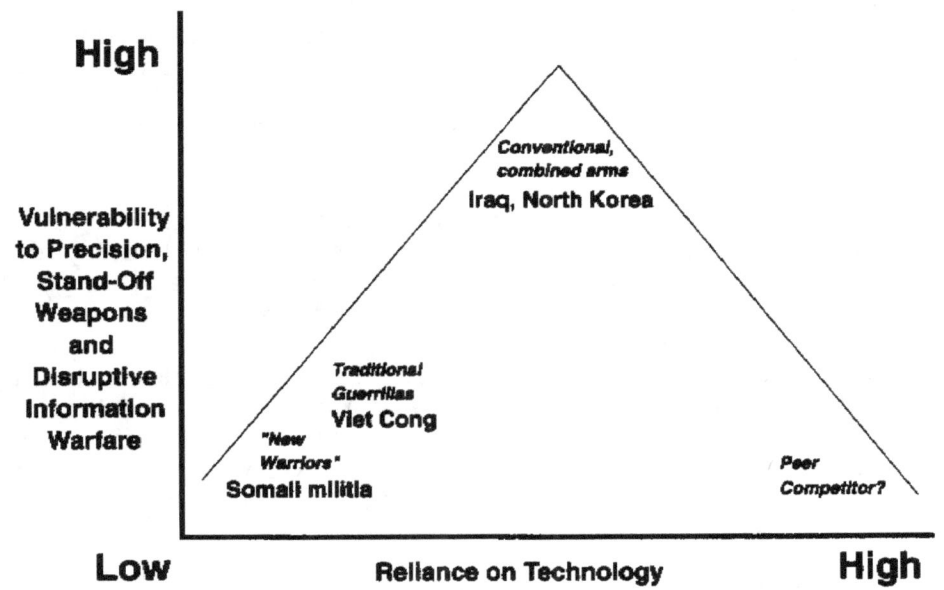

Figure 6. Utility of Current Revolution.

19

eroding the effectiveness and morality of stand-off strikes. If they are terrorists, they need only succeed in a limited number of military missions to attain desired psychological objectives. To be popularly perceived a success, counterterrorism must be very nearly flawless. Even the RMA does not promise such perfection. While it may be argued that a non-RMA force suffers these same deficiencies, this overlooks the resource opportunity cost to design, create, and field a RMA force.

A second risk is that the greater the intensity with which the United States pursues the current RMA, the greater the intensity with which opponents or potential opponents will seek countermeasures. Potential competitors will no doubt respond to existing U.S. military preeminence. But such counter- measures are likely to take familiar forms against which superior U.S. training and capabilities can prevail if hostilities result. U.S. pursuit of revolutionary capabilities will produce a search for asymmetric countermeasures, including perhaps new biological and chemical weapons. Or American pursuit of the current RMA could actually encourage the emergence of a peer competitor, either by developing a *Dreadnought*-type weapon that instantly outmodes all previous systems, or by inspiring fear of what the United States intends to do with its increasing military capabilities among technologically-capable, but currently nonhostile, states.

Yet another risk is that fruition of the current RMA might lead the United States to overreliance on the military element of national power. This would be especially tempting if the global economic position of the United States continues to erode. But as Napoleon, Hitler and others discovered, military dominance is a deadly siren when it causes leaders to ignore political and economic power, leaving no foundation when military preeminence fades (as it invariably does). If this happens, the current RMA may prove less a groundwork for a more permanent world order than a temporary expedient for keeping the dogs of war at bay.

Finally, there is the risk that overly vigorous pursuit of the current RMA might increase problems with friends and allies. Advocates contend the RMA will make the U.S. military capable of successful, autonomous operations, and thus less dependent on allies. This would be a mixed blessing. The 19th century French social theorist Auguste Comte speculated that prehistoric humans developed the economic division of labor as a means of preserving social peace. Individuals reliant on the skills of others are less likely to do violence to them. The same may hold for the global system. Other nations would probably consider a U.S. military freed from dependence on allies much more dangerous than the pre-RMA one, thus tainting all aspects of cooperation.

Why, then, should the United States actively pursue the current RMA? First, it should bring significant increases in combat effectiveness against some mid-level opponents. Second, as many analysts have pointed out, a force built around stand-off, precision weapons and disruptive information warfare capabilities would, because of decreased friendly casualties and reduced collateral damage, be more politically usable than a traditional force-projection military. Third, by removing some of the fetters on the use of American military power, the RMA could augment deterrence. Other than the Soviet Union, every recent enemy of the United States has been militarily inferior, but many of them, from Ho Chi Minh to Saddam Hussein, thought that political constraints would counterbalance the U.S. military advantage. Such aggressors might be deterred more easily if a 21st century U.S. military could bypass or minimize certain types of political constraints. Despots would thus be assured that aggression would be punished. Finally, the United States may need to pursue the current RMA to avoid stumbling into strategic inferiority. The lead time for developing a new military based on the RMA is great. Technological development is the easy part; reshaping attitudes and adapting organizations, doctrine, education, and training is extraordinarily hard. When other states pursue revolutionary military developments, the United States must also.

If policymakers decide to enthusiastically pursue the revolution in military affairs, strategy, rather than technological capability, must be the lodestar. Over and over, American leaders and defense experts should ask "What do we want the future U.S. military to be able to do?" rather than "What will emerging technology allow the future military to do?" One way to think about what the 21st century U.S. military should be able to do is to examine a combination of strategic objectives and expected opponents.

Macro-level strategic objectives fall on a spectrum of engagement. At one end is creation of a global system composed exclusively of stable, prosperous, free-market democracies. At the other end is political and military disengagement with focus on internal problems. In the middle lies the current mixture of promoting democracy when possible at a low cost, containing aggressors, and pursuing special political and economic relationships in key regions such as Latin America, Western Europe, and the Pacific Rim. Where future U.S. strategy falls on this spectrum has tremendous implications for the sort of military force the nation needs. The more the United States stresses active engagement and the promulgation of open economies and political systems, the more the U.S. military must be able to project power and sustain protracted operations. To build democracy might require soldiers on the ground for extended periods of time while the institutions and values that support democracy are planted and take root. Large-scale strategic mobility would remain vital. Military strategy would combine precise, stand-off strikes with occupation and nation-building. Occupation forces would be armed largely with nonlethal weaponry and protected by high-tech armor and personal communications equipment.

By contrast, the more that the United States pursues political and military disengagement, the less the need for power projection or sustained operations. At this end of the spectrum, the appropriate military force would be configured for defense and short deterrent strikes. There would still be a need for precision, stand-off weapons systems. In fact, stand-off capability would be even more relevant since the United States would seldom operate with allies and would lack forward bases. There would be little need, though, to deploy and sustain occupying or nation-building forces. Strategic objectives in the middle of the spectrum would require power projection and deterrence, but occupation and nation-building functions might often be shared or done by allies. Alternatively, the United States could choose strategic objectives exclusively in concert with other members of the global community. As military forces become more expensive, the United States might decide that possession of a full range of capabilities is not worth the cost. This could lead to a global military division of labor, with the U.S. military always operating in coalition and thus needing only certain capabilities such as intelligence and information warfare rather than a full range.

The threats expected in the 21st century will also have a major effect on force development. When crafting an assessment of future threats, it again makes sense to think in terms of a spectrum.[43] At one end would be a peer competitor, or perhaps a coalition of complementary niche competitors organized along high-technology RMA lines. Next would be regional aggressors with large but less-developed military forces. Most of these would have weapons of mass destruction deliverable via ballistic or cruise missiles. They would also have some high-tech capabilities such as the ability to wage limited space operations and information warfare. Next on the spectrum would be subnational threats such as ethnic militias and terrorist movements. Some of these will remain primitive and rely on the traditional guerrilla tools of small arms, rocket propelled grenades, mortars, and mines, but many will have adopted a fair amount of emerging technology. In fact, some of them may be as advanced in their chosen form of combat as the U.S. military and thus constitute niche threats, particularly in forms of combat that do not require large numbers of participants like information warfare. The final pole of the spectrum will include essentially nonmilitary challengers that U.S. policymakers define as security threats. Most of these will be criminal organizations of one type or the other, some using traditional methods of violence, others relying on economic subversion, ecological terrorism or information warfare.[44]

The United States is likely to confront all of these types of enemies at one time or another in the coming decades. Force development must thus be driven by some projected priority among the threat types. The specific priority of expected enemies determines the specific types of military technology that should be stressed, the number of systems needed, the requirement for forces to perform sustained operations, whether mobilization will be a factor or whether all wars will be "come as you are," and the relationship of the U.S. military to nonmilitary security forces such as law enforcement agencies. Most current programs, including the Army's Force XXI, focus on conventional regional aggressors and, to a lesser extent, subnational enemies. From this perspective, stress on precision, stand-off strikes, stealth, and coherent operations is logical. But if the future threat set changes, these characteristics might not be the most important ones for the future U.S. military.

A peer competitor with armed forces as advanced as the U.S. military (although perhaps not in precisely the same way) could pose entirely different problems. Some optimists argue that in the future, wars can be won by crashing the enemy's computers rather than killing his soldiers and civilians. Unfortunately, the current revolution in military affairs does not rule out other, more deadly forms of combat. Warfare between advanced opponents could lead to bloody, World War I-like stalemate. Weapons could be so accurate and destructive that any emission of an electronic signature would draw an attack. To turn on equipment would be to die.

RMA-based warfare involving peer competitors might also prove deadly to civilians. Many analysts believe future war will resemble the stylized combat of medieval and 18th century Europe or pre-colonial Mesoamerica in which highly-trained warriors fought each other but usually did not kill civilians or lay waste to the lands of the defeated.[45] But if a revolution in military affairs is combined with hate, whether based on ethnicity, race, class, religion, ideology or some other factor, technology could be harnessed to the complete and utter annihilation of enemies, both civilian and military. Even societies "modern" enough to master a revolution in military affairs have not transcended the ability to hate, so salt could be plowed into the land a thousand times more effectively and efficiently than in ancient times. Coventry, Shanghai, Warsaw, Dresden, Hiroshima and a dozen other cities remind us of the depths that civilized states reach when hate, frustration, and technology combine.

Since such a war against a peer competitor would probably not be decided by traditional systems such as armored land forces and manned aircraft, to prepare for it the United States should shift toward second stage technologies such as robotics, psychotechnology, space domination, and "fire ant" capabilities. And, since projection of conventional forces against a peer competitor would be dangerous or impossible, in a direct confrontation with such a foe the United States should concentrate on projection of effects rather than objects. During competition with a peer adversary, the United States would certainly need a tightly integrated military-scientific-technological-economic policy aimed at limiting the proliferation of military-relevant knowledge. Finally, the line between competition and hostilities, between peace and war, may be extremely difficult to determine-particularly in the information arena. This implies a military capable of *continuous* defensive action rather than one configured for episodic offensive employment.

Rather than peer warfare, what used to be called low-intensity conflict could pose the dominant threat in the 21st century. Many writers have suggested this. In his seminal work, *The Transformation of War*, Martin van Creveld argues, "war will not be waged by armies but by groups whom we today call terrorists, guerrillas, bandits, and robbers, but who will undoubtedly hit on more formal titles to describe themselves."[46] Similarly, Ralph Peters considers the major threat to U.S. security to be challenges ranging from "techno-capable crime networks to the machete-swinging clans of warlords."[47] A U.S. military configured exclusively for use against subnational or nonmilitary enemies would look very different from the projected Force XXI. Individual units would be small but very flexible, able to deal with enemies with a tremendous range of capabilities, from high-tech niche opponents to low-tech warlord militias. In fact, the entire combat arms component of the Army might be composed of Special Forces. Small units, however, would not necessarily equate to a small total force, since defeating this type of opponent tends to be people-intensive, time-consuming and requires protracted commitment of forces. There would be little or no distinction between the military and nonmilitary elements of the U.S. security force. High-tech policemen and scientists, whether computer experts, ecologists, or something similar would be the most vital parts of the security force with soldiers as adjuncts. And, since the American public considers conflict short of war a low-stakes effort not worth extensive casualties, personal protection technology including individual armor and counterterror technology would be essential. Psycho-technology to manipulate perceptions, beliefs and attitudes would also be central. Some elements of the current RMA like long range, stealth, and space domination would count for little.

Tasks.

The RMA is at a crossroads. In the broadest sense, there are three options: to push further along the road of precision, stand-off strikes and disruptive information warfare aimed primarily at conventionally-armed regional aggressors; to put a brake on the RMA and stand pat in order to consolidate existing advantages; or, to push the revolution in a different direction. To structure this choice, the U.S. military must do a number of things. First, it must inspire and lead continued refinement of the theory of military revolutions. Second, it must examine how to cultivate internal creativity. Third, it must expand the debate.

To refine the theory of military revolutions, hypotheses should debated, revised, confirmed, or abandoned. Three issues in particular warrant further attention: the likely response of other states, second order effects, and the ability to respond across the spectrum of possible requirements (the "band-width problem").

In considering the response of other states, policymakers and defense planners consistently overlook or ignore the fact that U.S. power can be intimidating. Because Americans consider their intentions benign and their stated goals- democracy and free market economies-so clearly desirable, they fail to understand that even free market democracies can be unsettled by increases in U.S. military capability.[48] Why, foreign leaders ask, would the world's only superpower seek radical improvement of its armed forces in the absence of a clear threat? Given the expense of accumulating national power, some may assume it is meant to be used and conclude that the United States is improving its military capabilities in order to impose its will on others. The United States can either accept such suspicions or find a new, less intimidating method of pursuing the revolution in military affairs, perhaps through greater cooperation with potential allies. The problem is that such cooperation could speed the dissemination of new technology, techniques, and ideas, and thus contribute to the emergence of challengers. But if the United States unilaterally pursues the RMA, other states will respond, whether symmetrically or asymmetrically. In turn, knowing the benign intentions of the United States, American leaders and planners will consider this threatening. Why, they will ask, would other states seek to improve their military capability unless contemplating aggression? Vigorous American pursuit of the RMA may make other nations feel less secure and their response will make the United States feel less secure. The result may be a spiral of mutual misperception and a new arms race, albeit a qualitative rather than quantitative one. American policymakers must decide whether this is a cost worth bearing.

The second order effects of the RMA also warrant additional study. It is possible, for instance, that the RMA might lead to methods of warfighting incompatible with the ethos and tradition of the U.S. military. One example concerns training. Throughout history, military training has consisted of three interlinked dimensions, each focused on a different relationship (see Figure 7). To a large extent, drill dealt with a soldier's relationship with his comrades; discipline dealt with his relationship with superiors; simulation or actual combat practice dealt with his relationship with the enemy. The RMA may replicate medieval warfare where training focused on simulation to the almost-total exclusion of drill and discipline (but without even the modicum of control given medieval warfare by the code of chivalry). But if all training becomes simulation or wargaming, can armed forces still be disciplined and bonded into effective units? Will they need to be? The

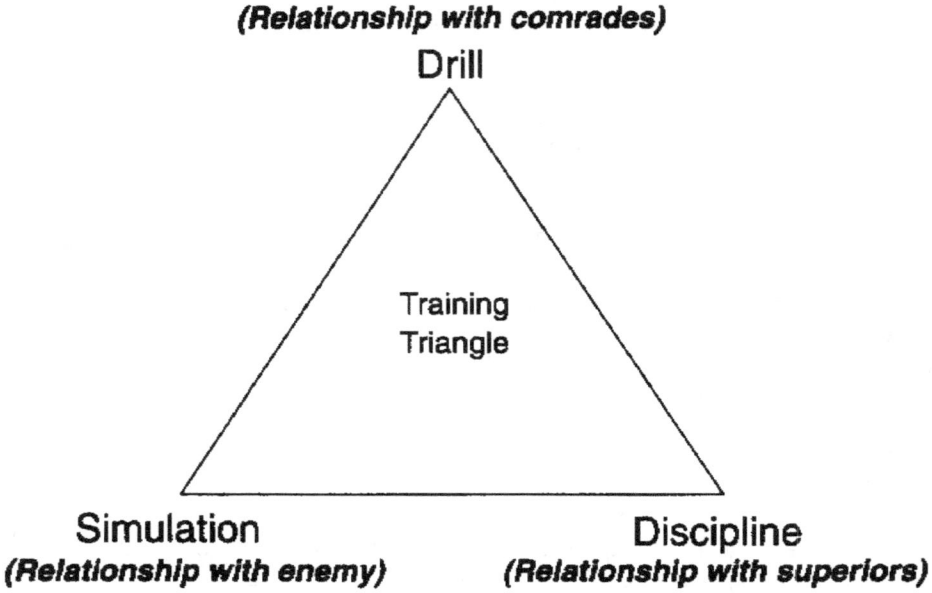

(Relationship with comrades)

Drill

Training
Triangle

Simulation | Discipline
(Relationship with enemy) | **(Relationship with superiors)**

Figure 7. Elements of Training.

answer to both questions may be "no." In fact, if warfighting is done from a computer terminal, it may not be necessary to have distinct military forces instilled with discipline and personal bravery.[49] In any case, the implications of this should b e explored *before* the point of no return.

The RMA may also have unintended and undesired second order effects on American society. One of the primary objectives of the RMA is near-omniscience for military commanders. Sensor and information-processing technology may give them full and instantaneous access to information on both their own and enemy soldiers. Commanders will know not only where their forces and those of the enemy are located, but also their physical and mental condition. And psychotechnology will allow commanders to manipulate the perceptions and beliefs of their own soldiers, the enemy, and noncombatants. Such capabilities could be used a s easily for domestic problems as for international ones, thus challenging fundamental American beliefs about personal privacy and the intrusion of the state in the lives of individuals. Is the nation

28

willing to accept the risk of an RMA pandora's box? If not, how can it avoid a spillover from the RMA to domestic society?

The U.S. military must also examine the band-width problem of the current RMA. A band-width problem arises when a military force is so focused on one particular type of opponent that it can be defeated by a different kind. During most of the Middle Ages, for example, the only true threat to a well-armored, well-mounted, and well-trained knight was another knight. By the 15th century, knights at Agincourt and other battles were devastated by formerly insignificant types of opponents such as archers, halberdiers, pikemen, and, later, arquebusiers. This problem has haunted militaries throughout history, from British Redcoats trumped by the "uncivilized" tactics of French, Indian, and American opponents to Iraqi forces trained and configured for war with Iran. In fact, the U.S. military experienced its own band-width problem a few decades ago. During the Eisenhower administration, the United States, as it assumed global responsibilities associated with the containment of communism, sought a technological solution to the expense of standing armed forces. The strategy of "massive retaliation" used American superiority in nuclear weapons and strategic airpower to offset the Soviets' advantage in conventional military force.[50] By the late 1950s, a band-width problem emerged and the U.S. military was ill-equipped for guerrilla conflict or for regional expeditionary warfare during crises such as the Bay of Pigs invasion.[51]

Most contemporary plans for the evolution of the U.S. military, such as the Army's Force XXI, focus on conventional, armor-heavy enemies.[52] Emergence of a band-width problem early in the next century is likely if United States confronts low-tech, niche, or peer opponents. While official documents note that "the Army must expand its understanding of conflict beyond current Western paradigms,"[53] most descriptions of how the "digitized" Army of the 21st century expects to fight sound suspiciously like armored combat against the Warsaw Pact with new technology grafted on.[54] Since, in Daniel Bolger's words, militaries tend to prepare for "the last *good* war," it is not surprising that current plans for the future of the U.S. military foresee Iraq-like opponents.[55] But American defense planners must recognize that even if the Gulf War and Force XXI do represent *a* revolution in military affairs, they may not represent *the* revolution. As the French discovered in 1940, improving the structure that brought victory in the last war does not guarantee victory in the next. It is not yet clear whether the United States is pursuing the right revolution. It is possible that policymakers, analysts, and planners are concentrating on the current "minor" RMA while ignoring the implications of the potential, even if more distant, "major" one. Historically, "minor" RMAs have had significant impact on battlefield effectiveness, but "major" RMAs have proven greater impediments to attainment of strategic objectives. It is far easier to determine a successful countermeasure to *blitzkrieg* than to the industrialization of war. And there is the danger, in A.J. Bacevich's words, that "the phenomena preoccupying us today may be mere blips distracting attention from other deeper currents of change."[56]

Refining the theory of military revolutions is not enough. The U.S. military and the Department of Defense must also discover how to better cultivate and reward creativity and organizational entrepreneurialism-to find the revolutionaries to lead the revolution. The military does not lack visionaries. As the Tofflers note, "For all the conservatism of military institutions, there have always been innovators calling for revolutionary change."[57] In the future, successful militaries must cultivate and preserve visionaries during noncrisis periods and empower them during crises. Within the contemporary U.S. military, visionaries are given voice in the service journals. But the probing creativity seen in *Parameters, Airpower Journal, Joint Forces Quarterly* and similar fora is counterbalanced by force development programs that assume constancy in the type of threats and the nature of U.S. objectives.

Admittedly, the time is not ripe for a full-blown, revolutionary transformation of the U.S. military. Toleration of visionaries is probably the best that can be expected in today's security environment. The key is developing the ability to know when it is time to empower them. Anyone looking at European military thinking between the world wars would have assumed that the

British or French would have been the masters of the new forms of warfare. The conceptual writings of people like Charles DeGaulle, B.H. Liddell Hart and J.F.C. Fuller outshone those of their German counterparts. But the Germans, unlike the British, empowered their visionaries and allowed them to restructure doctrine, tactics, training, and all the other elements of military art. In 1940 the British and French discovered that tolerating eccentricity is not the same as cultivating vision. The current U.S. military is dangerously close to the same trap. As Bacevich puts it, "Pretending to stride confidently toward the future, a military establishment fixated by revolution is more truly engaged in an effort to evade the past."[58] To avoid this, the United States must recognize that there may come a time when essentially evolutionary developments like the current Force XXI program are not enough and more radical ideas must be given effect.

Until then, the military should institutionalize creative thinking about the revolution in military affairs. This will require a conceptual locomotive to draw on the intellectual power of the military services without being their uncritical servant. It is difficult to pull an officer from a mainstream career and ask him to support ideas that obviate everything he has done. How easily can an armor officer, for instance, advocate an Army without tanks knowing that in the near future he will return to an institution where tanks are central? The same holds for fighter pilots, submarine captains or any other sort of officer. So long as they are part of a conventional institution, their creativity is constrained.[59] A new, autonomous RMA organization-if composed of analysts rather than advocates- could do what RAND Corporation did for nuclear strategy in the 1950s.[60] While affiliated with the Department of Defense, it should be staffed by a mix of civilians, officers on limited tours who will return to their services, and active and retired officers who spend the remainder of their career in the development and implementation of the revolution in military affairs.[61]

Finally, the military must enlarge the RMA debate. German strategy between 1871 and 1918 showed the danger of separating military strategy and force development from broader national policy.[62] Yet that is what is happening in the

United States today. Every analysis of the RMA originates from the military or from civilians with ties to the armed services. The 21st century U.S. military should be designed to attain specific objectives given a specific threat set. The military can participate in broadening the debate over national objectives. It can inform and inspire, perhaps even lead the effort. It cannot and should not do it alone. The military must, then, draw political leaders and the informed public into discussion of the RMA.

****

Strategic thinking occurs in three dimensions. The *vertical* dimension deals with time. Its grist is speculation about the future and balancing short-term and long-term objectives. Analysts of the RMA have given this a fair amount of attention. The *horizontal* dimension seeks to integrate and synchronize various types of power in a collective effort at a given point in time. There is little of this in the current RMA literature: few writers have explored the links between a military designed around the RMA and diplomatic or economic power. This can and should be done, but is not the most complex task. The third dimension of strategy is the *normative*. However much political realists deny it, strategy is about preferences, about value judgements, about not just the type of world that is *attainable*, but also what is *preferable*. With the exception of the Tofflers' undeveloped notion of "anti-war," explicit normative choices have been almost entirely absent from analysis of the RMA. If the United States is to lead and master the revolution rather than be its eventual victim, this vacuum must be filled. American leaders, in other words, must decide not only what the United States *can* do with a more effective military force, but also what it *should* do. Only then will the RMA lead to progress rather than simply change.

ENDNOTES

1. John M. Shalikashvili, *National Military Strategy of the United States: A Strategy of Flexible and Selective Engagement*, Washington, DC: Joint Staff, February 1995, pp. ii-iii.

2. Posted at World Wide Web site *http:// www.dtic.dla.mil/ defenselink/ jcs/ vice_chairman.html*.

3. Andrew W. Marshall, "Some Thoughts on Military Revolutions – Second Version," Memorandum for the Record, Office of the Secretary of Defense, Office of Net Assessment, August 23, 1993, p. 3.

4. Jeffrey R. Cooper, *Another View of the Revolution in Military Affairs*, Carlisle Barracks, PA: U.S. Army War College, Strategic Studies Institute, 1994, p. 27.

5. For example, Michael J. Mazarr, Jeffrey Shaffer, and Benjamin Ederington, *The Military Technical Revolution: A Structural Framework*, final report of the CSIS Study Group on the MTR, Washington, DC: Center for Strategic and International Studies, 1993; Dan Gouré, "Is There a Military-Technical Revolution in America's Future?" *Washington Quarterly*, Vol. 16, No. 4, Autumn 1993, pp. 175-192; and, John W. Bodnar, "The Military Technical Revolution: From Hardware to Information," *Naval War College Review*, Vol. 46, No. 3, Summer 1993, pp. 7-21.

6. An exception is Kenneth F. McKenzie, Jr., "Beyond Luddites and Magicians: Examining the MTR," *Parameters*, Vol. 25, No. 2, Summer 1995, pp. 15-21. The author does not explain why he uses a term or concept that has largely been abandoned by other analysts.

7. Civilian analysts tend toward "underway." Military officers, perhaps inherently more conservative, see more "evolution" than "revolution" in current events, but readily acknowledge that the future implications of silicon-chip and other advanced technologies may be revolutionary. See, for example, *The U.S. Air Force Roundtable on the Revolution in Military Affairs,* McLean, VA: Science Applications International Corporation, January 1994; *The U.S. Navy Roundtable on the Revolution in Military Affairs,* McLean, VA: Science Applications International Corporation, July 1994; *The Summary Roundtable on the Revolution in Military Affairs,* McLean, VA: Science Applications International Corporation, October 1994.

8. Alvin and Heidi Toffler, *War and Anti-War: Survival at the Dawn of the 21st Century,* Boston: Little, Brown, 1993, p. 32.

9. Robert J. Bunker, "The Transition To Fourth Epoch War," *Marine Corps Gazette*, Vol. 78, No. 9, September 1994, pp. 20-34.

10. Cooper, *Another View of the Revolution in Military Affairs*, p. 21.

11. Andrew F. Krepinevich, "Cavalry to Computer: The Pattern of Military Revolutions," *The National Interest*, No. 37, Fall 1994, p. 30.

12. Krepinevich, "Cavalry to Computer," p. 30; Cooper, *Another View of the Revolution in Military Affairs*, p. 1; in addition, each of the Department of Defense-sponsored service roundtables on the RMA were organized around these four elements. (See *The U.S. Army Roundtable on the Revolution in Military Affairs,* McLean, VA: Science Applications International Corporation, October 1993; *The U.S. Air Force Roundtable on the Revolution in Military Affairs*; *The U.S. Navy Roundtable on the Revolution in Military Affairs*; *The Summary Roundtable on the Revolution in Military Affairs*.)

13. James R. Fitzsimonds and Jan M. Van Tol, "Revolutions in Military Affairs," *Joint Force Quarterly*, No. 4, Spring 1994, p. 27.

14. The "First Wave" was agricultural, the "Second Wave" industrial. Alvin and Heidi Toffler, *War and Anti-War: Survival at the Dawn of the 21st Century,* Boston: Little, Brown, 1993, pp. 33-85. See also Alvin and Heidi Toffler, *The Third Wave*, New York: Bantam, 1980.

15. See, for example, Pat Cooper, "Information Warfare Sparks Security Affairs Revolution," *Defense News*, Vol. 10, No. 23, June 12-18, 1995, p. 1.

16. See, for instance, George J. Stein, "Information Warfare," *Airpower Journal*, Vol. 9, No. 1, Spring 1995, pp. 30-55; Edward Mann, "Desert Storm: The First Information War?" *Airpower Journal*, Vol. 8, No. 4, Winter 1994, pp. 4-14; and, Owen Jensen, "Information Warfare: Principles of Third-Wave War," *Airpower Journal*, Vol. 8, No. 4, Winter 1994, pp. 35-44.

17. For intra-military discussion, see *The US Air Force Roundtable on the Revolution in Military Affairs*. For beginning attempts to explore the strategic utilization of information warfare, see Tofflers, *War and Anti-War*; Arquilla and Ronfeldt, "Cyberwar is Coming!"; John Arquilla, "The Strategic Implications of Information Dominance," *Strategic Review*, Vol. 22, No. 3, Summer 1994, pp. 24-30; and Winn Schwartau, *Information Warfare: Chaos on the Electronic Superhighway*, New York: Thunder's Mouth Press, 1994.

18. Chris Morris, Janet Morris, and Thomas Baines, "Weapons of Mass Protection: Nonlethality, Information Warfare and Airpower in the Age of Chaos," *Airpower Journal*, Vol. 9, No. 1, Spring 1995, p. 27.

19. Thomas E. Ricks, "New Class of Weapons Could Incapacitate Foe Yet Limit Casualties," *Wall Street Journal*, January 4, 1993, p. 1.

20. Bradley Graham, "Use of Nonlethal Arms Leaves Pentagon Scrambling," *Washington Post*, February 24, 1995, p. 8.

21. In June 1993 the Defense and Arms Control Studies Program at the Massachusetts Institute of Technology sponsored a conference on the policy implications of nonlethal warfare technologies, but no major publications have yet grown from this. Harvey Sapolsky argues that in the search for nonlethal methods of warfare "isolationism will eventually be our answer." Harvey M. Sapolsky, "War without Killing," in Sam C. Sarkesian and John Mead Flanagin, eds., *U.S. Domestic and National Security Agendas*, Westport, CT: Greenwood Press, 1994, p. 39.

22. Edward N. Luttwak, "Toward Post-Heroic Warfare," *Foreign Affairs*, Vol. 74, No. 3, May/June 1995, p. 114.

23. Alan W. Debban, "Disabling Systems: War-Fighting Option for the Future," *Airpower Journal*, Vol. 7, No. 1, Spring 1993, p. 46.

24. Marshall, "Some Thoughts on Military Revolutions," p. 5.

25. Michael J. Mazarr, *The Revolution in Military Affairs: A Framework for Defense Planning*, Carlisle Barracks, PA: U.S. Army War College, Strategic Studies Institute, 1994.

26. Krepinevich, "Cavalry to Computer," p. 31.

27. See John A. Warden III, "The Enemy as a System," *Airpower Journal*, Vol. 9, No. 1, Spring 1995, pp. 40-55.

28. Martin C. Libicki, *The Mesh and the Net: Speculations on Armed Conflict in a Time of Free Silicon*, Washington, DC: National Defense University, Institute for National Strategic Studies, 1994, pp. 28-38.

29. An exception is Ralph Peters who writes, "The latest 'Revolution in Military Affairs' occurred in the 1980s. It is over now." ("After the Revolution," *Parameters*, Vol. 25, No. 2, Summer 1995, p. 7.)

30. While the Tofflers' linkage of economic and modes of warfare is certainly accurate, their understanding of economic and military history is occasionally thin as, for instance, when they attribute the Napoleonic revolution to industrialization despite the fact that the Emperor's arms were made with the same technology that had been used to equip the armies of Marlborough. Probably a better schema links the military revolution of the 16th and 17th centuries–the predominance of gunpowder, square-rigged ships with artillery in broadside, drilled standing armies, and the like–with the transition from a feudal to commercial economy, while the military revolution of the late 19th century resulted from industrialization and the first stage of the technological revolution.

31. Interestingly, by the early 20th century, maturation of the bolt-action rifle technology restored the importance of superior training and

discipline–as the "Old Contemptibles" of the BEF were able to demonstrate at Mons and Le Cateau in 1914. By then, of course, other advances had made deciding the issue of a great power conflict via infantry weapons unlikely. See William McElwee, *The Art of War: Waterloo to Mons*, Bloomington: Indiana University Press, 1975.

32. Russell F. Weigley, *The Age of Battles: The Quest for Decisive Warfare from Breitenfeld to Waterloo*, Bloomington: Indiana University Press, 1991, p. xv.

33. Robert L. O'Connell, *Of Arms and Men: A History of War, Weapons, and Aggression*, New York: Oxford University Press, 1989, p. 40.

34. John Keegan, *A History of Warfare*, New York: Alfred A. Knopf, 1993, pp. 168, 238; Michael Howard, "The Military Factor in European Expansion," in Hedley Bull and Adam Watson, eds., *The Expansion of International Society*, Oxford: Clarendon, 1984.

35. For discussions of the German Army's development of *Blitzkrieg,* see Charles Messenger, *The Blitzkrieg Story*, New York: Scribner, 1976; Len Deighton, *Blitzkrieg: From the Rise of Hitler to the Fall of Dunkirk*, New York: Knopf, 1980; and Byran Perrett, *A History of Blitzkrieg*, New York: Stein & Day, 1983.

36. See Robert A. Doughty, *The Seeds of Disaster: The Development of French Army Doctrine, 1919-1939*, Hamden, CT: Archon, 1985.

37. Krepinevich, "Cavalry to Computer," p. 40; Marshall, "Some Thoughts on Military Revolutions," p. 3.

38. Hajo Holborn, "The Prusso-German School: Moltke and the Rise of the General Staff," in Peter Paret, ed., *Makers of Modern Strategy from Machiavelli to the Nuclear Age*, Princeton, NJ: Princeton University Press, 1986, pp. 281-284.

39. John Keegan, *The Price of Admiralty: The Evolution of Naval Warfare*, New York: Viking, 1989, pp. 100-122.

40. B.H. Liddell Hart, *Strategy*, 2d revised edition, New York: Signet, 1974; Edward N. Luttwak, *Strategy: The Logic of War and Peace*, Cambridge, MA: Belknap, 1987.

41. The German attacks against both France and Russia during World War II can be viewed in this light. Although the German military made some arguments against initiating both campaigns when they did, Hitler strongly felt that Germany's advantage in military capability would only erode as time passed.

42. The Air Force Roundtable on the RMA, after extensive consideration of the targeting problem, concluded "While technology will increasingly allow us to identify and target specific aim points, one thing that has never changed, and that technology is likely not to change, is the importance of knowing where and when to aim." *The U.S. Air Force Roundtable on the Revolution in Military Affairs*, n.p.

43. Similarly, the U.S. Navy RMA Roundtable conferees concluded: "The focus . . . should be less on identifying any *particular* state as the most likely future challenger, and more on the characteristics and capabilities of the *kinds* of states likely to pose a challenge." (italics in original) *The U.S. Navy Roundtable on the Revolution in Military Affairs*, n.p.

44. On the vulnerability of the United States to nonmilitary information warfare, see Schwartau, *Information Warfare*.

45. Luttwak, "Toward Post-Heroic Warfare."

46. Martin van Creveld, *The Transformation of War*, New York: Free Press, 1991, p. 197.

47. Peters, "After the Revolution," pp. 8, 9.

48. On this point, American liberalism is a less sophisticated ideology than Soviet Marxism-Leninism, which at least understood that there are powerful elites with vested interests who will oppose the spread of "equality and justice." Americans remain perplexed at elites who oppose the spread of free market democracy.

49. An interesting perspective on many of these issues can be found in Orsan Scott Card, *Ender's Game*, New York: Tom Doherty, 1985.

50. For detail, see Steven Metz, "Eisenhower and the Planning of American Grand Strategy," *Journal of Strategic Studies*, Vol. 14, No. 1, March 1991, pp. 49-71.

51. See Maxwell D. Taylor, *The Uncertain Trumpet*, New York: Harper and Brothers, 1959.

52. The latest thinking on the Army's Force XXI process can be found at World Wide Web site *http://204.7.227.67:1100/force21*.

53. TRADOC (Training and Doctrine Command) Pamphlet 525-5, *Force XXI Operations*, August 1994, n.p. (electronic download).

54. For example, Bernard Gray, "Digital Troops on the Horizon," *London Financial Times*, May 19, 1995, p. 11.

55. Daniel P. Bolger, "The Ghosts of Omdurman," *Parameters*, Vol 21, No. 3, Autumn 1991, p. 32.

56. A.J. Bacevich, "Preserving the Well-Bred Horse," *The National Interest*, No. 37, Fall 1994, p. 49.

57. Tofflers, *War and Anti-War*, p. 29.

58. Bacevich, "Preserving the Well-Bred Horse," p. 49.

59. In a recent series of RMA roundtables, each of the individual services independently identified failure to create a climate or culture that "nurtures innovators, revolutionaries, or entrepreneurs" as an impediment to pursuit of the RMA. *The U.S. Army Roundtable on the Revolution in Military Affairs,* n.p; *The U.S. Air Force Roundtable on the Revolution in Military Affairs,* n.p; *The U.S. Navy Roundtable on the Revolution in Military Affairs,* n.p.

60. "There is a need for an organization free of current, day-to-day operational concerns and charged by OSD with developing R&D, training, operational, and other concepts to fit scenarios in the 2020 timeframe." *The U.S. Navy Roundtable on the Revolution in Military Affairs,* Tab F, n.p.

61. Perhaps distinguished flag officers on their last tour of duty. The Navy Board which fostered carrier and amphibious warfare in the 1920s and 1930s was just so composed. See W. Spencer Johnson, "Shifting Charts: The Navy and the Revolution in Military Affairs," in *The U.S. Navy Roundtable on the Revolution in Military Affairs,* n.p.

62. Holger H. Herwig, "Strategic Uncertainties of a Nation-State: Prussia-Germany, 1871-1918," in Williamson Murray, MacGregor Knox, and Alvin Bernstein, eds., *The Making of Strategy: Rulers, States, and War*, Cambridge: Cambridge University Press, 1994, pp. 242-277.

U.S. ARMY WAR COLLEGE

Major General Richard A. Chilcoat
Commandant

*****

STRATEGIC STUDIES INSTITUTE

Director
Colonel Richard H. Witherspoon

Director of Research
Dr. Earl H. Tilford, Jr.

Authors
Dr. Dr. Steven Metz
Lieutenant Colonel James Kievit

Editor
Mrs. Marianne P. Cowling

Secretary
Ms. Rita A. Rummel

*****

Composition
Mr. Daniel B. Barnett

Cover Artist
Mr. James E. Kistler

www.ingramcontent.com/pod-product-compliance
Lightning Source LLC
Chambersburg PA
CBHW080916290526
45795CB00007BA/2537